IMAGES
of America
LAGUNA BEACH

This beautiful aerial view of Laguna Beach truly captures the town's hidden quality, as it is nestled between rolling hills and a stunning coastline. With Saddleback Mountain in the background and the empty space of land in between, it is no wonder that Laguna Beach was a popular destination for new residents and visitors over 100 years ago. (Courtesy of Silver Images.)

ON THE COVER: Main Beach is Laguna's "Window to the Sea" and is located in the heart of downtown. (Courtesy of the Tom Pulley Postcard Collection.)

IMAGES
of America

LAGUNA BEACH

Claire Marie Vogel

ARCADIA
PUBLISHING

Published by Arcadia Publishing
Charleston, South Carolina

Library of Congress Control Number: 2008935200

For all general information contact Arcadia Publishing at:
Telephone 843-853-2070
Fax 843-853-0044
E-mail sales@arcadiapublishing.com
For customer service and orders:
Toll-Free 1-888-313-2665

Visit us on the Internet at www.arcadiapublishing.com

This book is dedicated to the Laguna Music collective—a diverse group of artists who give this town the completely unique culture I love.

A woman and her dog stand for a quick snapshot on their walk along Cliff Drive, a street that follows Heisler Park and overlooks the ocean. (Courtesy of the Brown family.)

CONTENTS

ACKNOWLEDGMENTS

This book would not be nearly as complete without the aid of Gene Felder of the Laguna Beach Historical Society. His help with accessing the images and facts of our town were an enormous gift to me, and I greatly appreciate the time he spent assisting me. An equally huge contributor to this book was Jim Nordstrom at Silver Images. Jim has an amazing collection of vintage Laguna Beach photographs. Thank you, Jim, for your friendship, guidance, and support. Thank you to Roger Jones for being so helpful, kind, and inspiring. I would also like to thank Karen and Steve Turnbull for their historical preservation of the town through great stories and outstanding photographs. Many local families and individuals contributed their time and historical images to this book. The Lansdell family sat with me for many hours sharing wonderful stories. Christian Marriner allowed me to use his family's captivating photographs. Thanks to Andy Alison for being so enthusiastic and for bringing the Marriners' collection to my attention. Janet Blake at the Laguna Art Museum provided me with the amazing Hurrell portraits of Laguna artists. Those pictures mean the world to me, and I am honored to be able to include them in this book. Thank you to Latitude 33 Bookshop for being a great environment for a first-time author and to Melony Vance for being the first to encourage me to write this book. Much appreciation goes to the Laguna Beach Public Library for their sizable photograph and book collections. Thank you to my family for being so supportive in this jump into something so different and exciting. The wonderful Cronin family gave me food, encouragement, photographs, chats, and everything else. Many thanks to Mikal Cronin for being my driver, second opinion, and helper for whatever I needed. Thanks go to Bob and Mary Phillips for being so sweet and welcoming. My gratitude goes to Tex Haines and everyone else at Victoria Skimboards who helped in the effort to get my hands on the amazing skimboarding photograph. Coast Hardware let everyone know about this book, putting up flyers and being altogether helpful. Thank you to everyone who contributed, called, e-mailed, or shared any support with me over the course of the book. Lastly a huge thanks goes to my editor, Jerry Roberts at Arcadia Publishing, for being so patient and understanding with my hectic schedule. Thank you!

INTRODUCTION

The area of Laguna Beach has been a popular destination for vacationers since the late 1800s. It began in 1870, when Eugene Salter traveled westward through the Aliso Canyon and became the first person to claim land in South Laguna under the Homestead Act. The act enabled Salter to claim 152 acres of government land where he built a one-room shack. Within the next two years, Salter abandoned his home and the 152 acres—one 8-acre corner of which ran down to the sea.

George and Sarah Thurston had been traveling with their children from Utah for close to nine months before coming to Laguna Beach in November 1871. George Thurston came through Laguna Canyon and found a fisherman on the shore. After inquiring about open government land, George was directed to Salter's cabin in Aliso Canyon and quickly decided to move his family there. The Thurston family claimed the abandoned homestead for themselves, set up a house, and planted various gardens and tree groves. To make money and obtain supplies, George Thurston traveled to Los Angeles, Santa Ana, and San Diego. Journeys to each of these distant cities from the homestead took many days.

The family's nearest neighbors were more than 10 miles away. Because the homestead was in the southern area of Laguna Beach, the Thurstons were cut off from what is now the main part of town and Laguna Canyon. The areas of what are now called Bluebird Canyon and Sleepy Hollow, in between the Thurstons and Laguna Canyon, were difficult to travel through, as horses could not manage the terrain. The family was not alone after a time, as the town eventually gained new homesteaders over the following years and visitors began to come more often.

Hotels were built and more people traveled to the town to enjoy the pleasant climate, stunning sights, and simple lifestyle. It was only natural that artists would soon be drawn to the town and its unique beauty. Art galleries, festivals, and more hotels came to the town, drawing added visitors every year. The city of Laguna Beach has remained a town of mostly independently owned stores, a small and close-knit population, as well as a village of art. Laguna Beach is a town unlike any other, and the citizens strive to keep it genuine and natural.

This very early photograph of Laguna Beach in the 1870s shows that Main Beach has been a favored destination since its discovery. (Courtesy of the Turnbull Collection.)

One

THE EARLY YEARS

Aliso Canyon is pictured in 1902. In 1870, Eugene Salter came through Aliso Canyon, claimed 152 acres of government land in South Laguna under the Homestead Act, and built a one-room shack. Within two years, Salter abandoned his home and the land. George and Sarah Thurston had been traveling with their children from Utah for close to nine months before coming to Laguna Beach. George was directed to Salter's cabin in Aliso Canyon and quickly decided to move his family there. The Thurstons claimed the abandoned homestead, set up a house, and planted various gardens and tree groves. Their nearest neighbors were over 10 miles away, and they were cut off from what is now the main part of town. The family was not alone forever, as the town gained new homesteaders over the following years and visitors began to come more often. (Courtesy of the Turnbull Collection/First American Title Corporation.)

A lone fisherman stands on Victoria Beach with Goff Island in the background. The rock formation was named after the early Laguna settler Hubbard Goff. (Courtesy of the Phillips family.)

The old road through the Laguna Canyon is pictured here in its most basic state. The stagecoach would come in from Santa Ana and through El Toro on this road to bring visitors into Laguna. (Courtesy of the Laguna Beach Historical Society.)

Thousand Steps Beach is pictured in the early 1920s and is desolate except for the footsteps in the sand. Thousand Steps Beach actually only has about 230 steps to the stairs in place now, but it is still a long and steep walk down. Because of its hidden access, it is a beach that is most often used by locals. (Courtesy of the Turnbull Collection/First American Title Corporation.)

The Thurston home is pictured along Aliso Creek. In the 1940s, a tract of 84 acres was purchased in Aliso Canyon for a golf course. In 1950, Laguna Beach Country Club opened, and it became the first golf course in Laguna Beach. There are plans underway to build a replicate version of the Thurston home in order to show people what it might be like to live on this beautiful land and to keep the memory alive of this important pioneer family. (Courtesy of the Turnbull Collection/ First American Title Corporation.)

This *c.* 1915 image shows the location of what is now Laguna Canyon Road going toward the ocean. The house pictured is the Harvey Hemenway homestead, which is sitting on what is now approximately the corner of Canyon Acres Drive and Arroyo Road. Hemenway came to Laguna Beach in a very unexpected way. After being abducted in San Francisco, he was forced onto a ship, which was to take him down to South America for slave labor. While aboard the ship, Hemenway saw some lights on the shores of Laguna, jumped the ship, and escaped to shore. Hemenway then homesteaded 500 acres of land in the 1890s and was said to have called it Canyon Acres, which evidently lead to the naming of the nearby road. (Courtesy of the Laguna Beach Historical Society.)

The early Mormon pioneer Andrew Wesley Thompson (center), his family (left), and the Starkey family (right) are pictured here in 1888. In 1876, Thompson and his family came to what was then called Lagona and purchased 172 acres. Thompson was a preacher of the Church of Latter-day Saints, and it is thought that his influence may have encouraged other Mormons to settle in Laguna Beach as well. (Courtesy of the Ramsey Collection.)

The home pictured here was built by the Mormon pioneer Andrew Wesley Thompson in Laguna Canyon. Around 1889, he moved the home to El Toro Road, where it was later demolished in 1966. (Courtesy of the Ramsey Collection.)

The early Mormon pioneers stayed in Laguna Beach for about 15 years until the 1890s, when people began to move away, jacking up their houses and taking them along. The only building that remained was this Mormon schoolhouse, which was built in the late 1880s and then abandoned in 1892. The school was moved to Canyon Acres Drive and Laguna Canyon Road, where it became a grammar school in 1893. In 1908, the Yoch family bought the building and moved it to Aliso Street, which is now Catalina Street, between Park and Legion Streets. The Yochs donated land and the building to become the first Catholic church in town, which was originally called St. Joseph's. (Courtesy of the Ramsey Collection.)

A family and their two dogs enjoy the empty Three Arch Bay in the 1920s. (Courtesy of the Turnbull Collection.)

The homestead of James Shrewsbury sits atop what is now Third Avenue in 1901. Many agriculturists practiced dry farming in Laguna Beach, because fresh water was often unavailable. Farmers in the area would generally grow beans and melons. (Courtesy of the Turnbull Collection.)

The children of Laguna Beach were educated in Legion Hall. Pictured here is the class of 1923. The boy on the far left is Howard Wilson, the son of South Laguna proprietor George Wilson. The girl sitting above him is Doris Thurston, and the boy in the top left corner is Mac Ropp, son of Laguna painter Roy Ropp. (Courtesy of the Turnbull Collection.)

A cheerful group is seen here fishing at Arch Beach in the early 1900s. (Courtesy of the Turnbull Collection/First American Title Corporation.)

The stagecoach comes through the bumpy Laguna Canyon around 1910. The Concord Stage was offered to travelers in the early days of Laguna as a way to get to the town from places like Santa Ana and El Toro. In the 1890s, the Concord Stage would often make the trip to Santa Ana about every other day. (Courtesy of the Turnbull Collection/First American Title Corporation.)

An early settler of Laguna Beach, Hubbard Goff, built this short-lived hotel in 1886. The property was near Diamond Street, and Hubbard called it the Arch Beach Hotel. The hotel stayed until the 1890s, when it was forced to close its doors. It was later added to Yoch's Laguna Beach Hotel. (Courtesy of Silver Images.)

The stagecoach driver was an honored position, especially of the Concord. William Brooks is pictured driving the simple stage with no springs, which instead swung in leather straps. The motion of this would often make riders sick. When cars replaced the coaches of Laguna, the stage was put on display in town. At one point, a man working for a film company bought it for $50. Sadly the historic stagecoach became an expendable prop, run off a cliff near Aliso Creek and, in the end, destroyed. (Courtesy of the Ramsey Collection.)

17

Mr. and Mrs. George Taylor built this beach house on an oceanfront lot at Arch Beach in 1887. The Taylors can be seen sitting in the cart to the right of the porch. (Courtesy of the Ramsey Collection.)

Main Beach was already proving to be a popular summer spot for vacationers in the early 1900s, as seen in this photograph. Visitors often traveled two days in a wagon to spend their summers in Laguna Beach. The tents would be pitched in different spots depending upon where that visitor was from. The Santa Ana travelers would usually locate themselves closer to Fisherman's Cove and Boat Canyon, whereas the Riverside residents would stay closer to Main Beach and the south. (Courtesy of the Ramsey Collection.)

A single house stands on the cliffs with a view of Victoria Beach and Goff Island in the background. If one looks closely, some white tents can be seen perched upon the cliffs by Goff Island. (Courtesy of the Phillips family.)

William H. Brooks built the Brooks Hotel in 1893. In this hotel were a grocery store, post office, and barbershop. Unfortunately, after just 60 days, the entire building burned down. The only thing that was not ruined was a ham that was thrown out of the grocery store window. (Courtesy of the Laguna Beach Historical Society.)

Joe Thurston's wagon would come into town and sell food, such as melons and vegetables from his garden in Aliso Canyon. Joseph came to Laguna Beach in 1871 with his family when he was only three years old. (Courtesy of the Ramsey Collection.)

The Thurston homestead is pictured in the 1930s in Aliso Canyon. The family cultivated wheat, corn, walnuts, grapes, peaches, apricots, prunes, plums, almonds, and watermelons and collected honey. (Courtesy of the Ramsey Collection.)

The old pier is pictured off of Main Beach in the late 1920s. The pier was built in 1926 from the area where the gazebo at Heisler Park stands now. It extended beyond the rocks so that coastal and fishing boats could tie up. The pier stood until 1939 when it was destroyed by a hurricane. (Courtesy of the Turnbull Collection/First American Title Corporation.)

This is the home that George Rogers built in the 1890s, known as "The Old Ranch House." In 1927, the Women's Club purchased the house, and in 1950, the property was bought to become the Laguna Beach City Hall. The historic pepper tree that stands in front of city hall is believed to have been planted by George Rogers back in the late 1800s. (Courtesy of the Turnbull Collection/ First American Title Corporation.)

The white building in the background is the house of early homesteader Nathaniel Brooks near what is now Ocean Avenue. (Courtesy of the Ramsey Collection.)

The area of Sleepy Hollow is pictured here, with Main Beach seen in the distance. (Courtesy of the Turnbull Collection/First American Title Corporation.)

The Isch Grocery store and U.S. post office sit among the ever-present eucalyptus trees near what are now Laguna Avenue and Coast Highway. The stagecoach would drop off travelers at Isch's store, where the first greeter, Old Joe Lucas, would wave and welcome the incoming crowds. (Courtesy of Silver Images.)

Main Beach is shown here in its earlier and calmer days. The Laguna Beach Hotel can be seen at the end of the line of cottages facing the ocean. (Courtesy of Silver Images.)

In the 1890s, when the hotel boom ended in Laguna Beach, Joseph Yoch purchased Hubbard Goff's Arch Beach Hotel and his brother Henry Goff's hotel, which was located on the oceanfront in downtown. Yoch had the Arch Beach Hotel broken down into three sections in order to be moved and connected to the hotel in the village. After joining these two hotels, Yoch ended up with a 30-room, two-bath building. This would be known as the Laguna Beach Hotel or sometimes as the Yoch Hotel. Many celebrities came to stay there and to relax on Laguna's shores. (Courtesy of Silver Images.)

The Laguna Beach Hotel gardens are pictured in 1910. (Courtesy of the Turnbull Collection/ First American Title Corporation.)

The development of Aliso Canyon is only slight in the year 1900. The Aliso Creek Beach became a very popular location for beachgoers and campers. (Courtesy of the Turnbull Collection.)

The Mormon schoolhouse that once stood in the Laguna Canyon is pictured between Park and Legion Streets in 1908 after being moved by the Yoch family. It was the first Catholic church in town and was originally named St. Joseph's. (Courtesy of the Ramsey Collection.)

The Aliso Beach tent camps were run by George Wesley Wilson, who rented space for 50¢ a day back in the 1920s. The nearby Wesley Drive and Wilson Street are named after the same Aliso View Grocery proprietor. (Courtesy of the Turnbull Collection.)

A stagecoach poses on main beach in front of the Laguna Beach Hotel, owned by Joseph Yoch until the 1930s, when it was sold and rebuilt to become the present-day Hotel Laguna. (Courtesy of the Turnbull Collection/First American Title Corporation.)

Josie Derkum Rice would meet her brother's fishing boat as it came in to shore and would help pull the boat and the catch to dry land, as pictured here in 1908. Josie was painted by noted artist Lewis Betts in 1914. Betts came to this coast to find and paint the *Girl of the Golden West*. Once he found Josie, he began painting her and her horse, Honda. The painting hangs in the Art Institute of Chicago when it is not being exhibited elsewhere in the United States. (Courtesy of the Ramsey Collection.)

The Seeman brothers built the Seeman Swinging Bridge at Arch Beach around 1914 so that people could access the rocks for fishing. (Courtesy of the Ramsey Collection.)

The Pomona College Marine Laboratory was built in 1913 on what is now the corner of Broadway Street and Coast Highway. The building was two stories high with concrete vats built into the floors. A pipe was connected to these vats, which then ran under the road to the ocean, where saltwater would be piped into the vats to keep the marine life alive so students could study it. In the 1930s, an advertisement in the local paper called attention to the college's Serpentarium, asking people to bring in mice, rats, gophers, and squirrels to which the bearer would be paid 1¢ or 2¢ depending on the size of the rodent. (Courtesy of the Turnbull Collection/First American Title Corporation.)

In response to the amount of students who were coming to Laguna Beach after the Pomona College Marine Laboratory was built in 1913, Howard Heisler decided to create accommodations. On the land he owned next to the college, which ran to Beach Street, Heisler erected 52 tents with wooden floors that were rented to students for $10 a week per tent. Each housed four people. (Courtesy of the Turnbull Collection/First American Title Corporation.)

This panoramic image shows the Pomona College, the tent city offices, and the refreshment

A car full of smiling beachgoers travels down Ocean Avenue in 1913. (Courtesy of Silver Images.)

stand, which are all facing Main Beach. (Courtesy of Silver Images.)

A father and his sons prepare for a day at Main Beach. (Courtesy of Silver Images.)

When Arch Beach Heights was subdivided in 1911, buyers mostly ignored it. At the time, the area was fairly difficult to access and seemingly cut off from the town. The prospective buyers that did come stayed at Ye Arch Beach Tavern, which was the official headquarters for the lot sales. The building was also used occasionally to house film crews and to shoot interior scenes. (Courtesy of Silver Images.)

A family stands in front of the sign for the Arch Beach Heights lot sales office, Ye Arch Beach Tavern, in the 1910s. (Courtesy of the Turnbull Collection.)

On Sundays, there were many activities to do in town. A popular event was horse racing. The horse racers would speed down Forest Avenue to Coast Highway. People would wager many things in place of money, like saddles, chaps, and even horses. This 1915 photograph features two men on horseback riding down the dirt road surrounded by eucalyptus trees on what is now Forest Avenue. (Courtesy of Silver Images.)

The Aliso View Grocery Store was owned and operated by George and Grace Wilson, who also ran the tent camp on Aliso Beach. The grocery store was built in 1922 and was located on the site of the present-day Montage Resort. (Courtesy of the Turnbull Collection.)

The town pavilion was used for everything, including church services, dances, weddings, funerals, and other town happenings. In the summer of 1918, Laguna Beach painter Edgar Payne conceived the idea of turning the town pavilion into an art gallery. Payne gathered local and visiting artists to create the Laguna Beach Art Association, and on July 27, 1918, the first Laguna art exhibition occurred. (Courtesy of the Laguna Beach Historical Society.)

Downtown Laguna Beach is seen at approximately Forest Avenue and Second Street. (Courtesy of the Ramsey Collection.)

In 1915, Carl Hofer opened an ice cream parlor on Forest Avenue. As a prize to the person who could suggest an adequate name for the store, he offered a leather pillow. A little girl stopped in and proposed to name it "The Gate," because her father had seen a pub in England with a gate sign that had poetry written on it. The girl won the pillow, and the now-historic hanging gate was made. It reads, "This gate hangs well and hinders none. Refresh and rest, then travel on." The gate exists today at the corner of Park and Forest Avenues at an ice cream parlor. (Courtesy of Silver Images.)

Herbert and Grace Rankin can be seen in the front of a car that is driving along Moss Point in South Laguna in 1910. Herbert Rankin operated the drugstore on Forest and Park Avenues in the 1930s. (Courtesy of the Turnbull Collection.)

To claim a homestead and as part of the Timber Culture Act, settlers were required to plant trees on cleared land in order to improve that land. Eucalyptus trees are fast growing and were once thought to be capable of many uses. Many of the planted Laguna eucalyptus trees grew up to 80 and 90 feet and ended up all over the town. (Courtesy of the Laguna Beach Historical Society/ First American Title Corporation.)

Women are seen in the early 1900s playing tennis near the Laguna Beach Hotel. (Courtesy of the Laguna Beach Historical Society/First American Title Corporation.)

A winding and unpaved coast road follows the ocean near Moss Point before the Coast Highway was made in 1926. (Courtesy of the Turnbull Collection/First American Title Corporation.)

The Irvine Bowl and Festival of Arts property is pictured here well before the spot was developed. A farmhouse, a windmill, and eucalyptus trees were the only landmarks around in the 1920s. (Courtesy of the Ramsey Collection.)

The beginnings of Pacific Coast Highway in South Laguna are pictured here as the highway is graded and prepared for pavement. The sign at right reads "Coast Royal," which is the name given to this section of South Laguna by the developer. (Courtesy of the Turnbull Collection.)

Two

THE INCORPORATED TOWN OF LAGUNA BEACH

Laguna Beach.

The Riviera of America.

Often referred to as the "Riviera of America," Laguna Beach gained much popularity in the 1920s. The town was officially incorporated on June 29, 1927. (Courtesy of Silver Images.)

Upon completion of the Pacific Coast Highway, a dedication ceremony was held in Laguna Beach. Academy Award–winning motion picture star Mary Pickford is at center surrounded by the small girls with the sashes. Pickford's husband, actor Douglas Fairbanks, is standing on the far left. (Courtesy of Silver Images.)

Some stylish women enjoy the view of the pier and sea in the 1920s. (Courtesy of Silver Images.)

Nathaniel Brooks purchased a used Imperial and provided the first auto service from Laguna Beach to Santa Ana. The driver of the car pictured is Nathaniel's nephew, Walter Brooks, around 1913. (Courtesy of the Ramsey Collection.)

The Laguna Beach Hotel stands on Coast Highway after 1926, when the dirt road was paved over. The hotel stands on the same site of the future Hotel Laguna, which replaced the Laguna Beach Hotel after it was demolished in the early 1930s. After the paving and widening of the highway, many eucalyptus trees were removed from the surrounding area. (Courtesy of the Laguna Beach Historical Society.)

The Orange County Historical Society visits the Laguna Beach Hotel in 1927. The society was established in 1919. (Courtesy of the Turnbull Collection/First American Title Corporation.)

Children play in the temperate summer water at Main Beach in 1915. (Courtesy of the Laguna Beach Historical Society.)

Main Beach in the 1920s was equipped with a bathhouse. (Courtesy of the Turnbull Collection/ First American Title Corporation.)

This photograph shows what Main Beach was like in its simpler times during the town's beginnings. (Courtesy of the Laguna Beach Historical Society.)

Main Beach is pictured on July 4, 1924, with the Cabrillo Ballroom and a boardwalk now added to the area. The ballroom was popular in the 1920s and 1930s, and many famous faces would show up to dance. Later on, the ballroom was converted into a bowling alley where playwright Tennessee Williams worked part-time as a pinsetter in the late 1930s. (Courtesy of the Laguna Beach Historical Society/First American Title Corporation.)

In the early 1930s, a group of businessmen purchased Joseph Yoch's Laguna Beach Hotel property for $84,000. The old hotel was then demolished and replaced by a new one. The early 1930s were not a good time for the economy, and businesses everywhere suffered. During the war years, the hotel was a home to marines and their families. In 1947, the furniture was purchased and new tenants arrived. The Hotel Laguna has been thriving ever since. (Courtesy of Silver Images.)

The rose garden on the side of the Hotel Laguna is a popular spot for events such as weddings. (Courtesy of the Marriner family.)

Laguna Beach greeter Eiler Larson (right) stands outside the Hotel Laguna to welcome visitors to the town. He would often wave at arrivals and holler, "Hello there!" (Courtesy of Silver Images.)

The Lumberyard is one of the most historic buildings in Laguna Beach today. The residents of Laguna in the early days would have to travel all the way to Santa Ana to get wood in order to build homes. Elmer Jahraus established the Lumberyard in 1912 in order to supply lumber to the town. The building has been used for various purposes since then but is currently a restaurant that has been named the Lumberyard in memory of its historic meaning to the town. (Courtesy of Silver Images.)

This single-wall-construction home on Sunset Terrace was built in 1936 and overlooks Victoria Beach. Many of the early cottages and bungalows of Laguna Beach were simple wood ones like this. The house, lot and all, was purchased for a mere $5,800 in the year it was constructed. (Courtesy of the Phillips family.)

Boat Canyon and Divers Cove are seen here with much of the area still in development. The road on the top going from left to right is North Coast Highway, and the road nearer to the bottom is Cliff Drive. (Courtesy of Silver Images.)

This panoramic image of the town shows Main Beach to North Coast Highway. (Courtesy of the

Elmer Brown's Boat Canyon home is pictured here around 1950 during its construction. The Cliff Drive home overlooks Fisherman's Cove, which is a popular spot for diving and viewing a wide array of fish and sea life. (Courtesy of the Brown family.)

Turnbull Collection/First American Title Corporation.)

Elmer Brown stands at his in-progress home at 650 Cliff Drive with his identically dressed sons. Pictured in 1950 from left to right are Bruce, Ted, Doug, and Elmer. Elmer established Laguna Travel Service, located on Broadway Street downtown. Doug, the oldest, took over the business later on. The travel service was sold in recent years but still runs today under different owners. (Courtesy of the Brown family.)

The Laguna Beach Fire Department sits next to city hall on Forest Avenue. The men pictured here in the 1930s are volunteer firefighters. The fire station was built in 1931. (Courtesy of Silver Images.)

The bus depot was located in downtown Laguna Beach. (Courtesy of Silver Images.)

The first U.S. post office in the town was given the official name of Lagona by the government. It stayed this way for 10 years, until 1904, when residents had the name changed to Laguna Beach, which they had been calling it for years. This 1940s Mediterranean Revival–style building served as the town's second post office. Located on Broadway Street in downtown Laguna, the building became unusable as a post office a few years after it was built due to traffic issues. The building still stands today. (Courtesy of the Laguna Beach Historical Society/Tom Pulley Postcard Collection.)

The men of the post office stand in front of their station on Broadway Street in the 1950s. The post office manager, Lloyd Babcock, was an oil painter who always kept the men busy. Until the mid-1950s, when the branch received trucks, the postmen walked everywhere carrying large, and often heavy, leather bags. (Courtesy of the Lansdell family.)

Bathers enjoy the view on the popular Main Beach in front of the Hotel Laguna in the 1950s. (Courtesy of the Laguna Beach Historical Society.)

This unique night shot of downtown in 1959 shows a pharmacy store off Main Beach and the Laguna South Coast Cinemas, located on South Coast Highway. The film listed on the marquee is Lana Turner's *Imitation of Life*. (Courtesy of Silver Images.)

Three

PEOPLE AND PLACES

Laguna Beach received its first greeter in the 1880s, when a Portuguese fisherman who people called Old Joe Lucas came to town. After surviving a shipwreck, Old Joe settled in Laguna Beach, where he could be seen at the Isch store greeting visitors coming in on the stagecoach and walking around with a Neptune-like trident. Old Joe Lucas knew very little English except when he swore, which was often and in English. Lucas passed away in 1908, and not until the 1940s did another greeter take over in welcoming visitors into Laguna. Eiler Larsen (pictured) traveled much of Europe and the United States before coming to Laguna, where he became the town's second greeter. Larsen would stand on Coast Highway hailing drivers and all else with a big "Hellooo!" Larsen did not have much money, but much of what he did have he spent on books, which he would later donate to libraries, and he also bought candy to hand out to children. (Courtesy of Silver Images.)

Various merchants of Laguna Beach are pictured in the 1920s. Joseph Thurston stands third from the left in the first row, artist Frank Cuprien stands second from the right in the first row, and Doris Messenger is at center in the sand. (Courtesy of the Laguna Beach Historical Society/First American Title Corporation.)

The Isch and Warling Palace Stable was co-owned by Nick Isch and Oscar Warling and was located across the Coast Highway from Forest Avenue. As times changed and cars became more prevalent than horses, the stables began servicing automobiles. (Courtesy of the Ramsey Collection.)

Joe Thurston is seen behind the reins of his horse-drawn cart. Joseph Thurston was only three when his family settled in Aliso Canyon. (Courtesy of Silver Images.)

The White House Restaurant was established in 1918 and remains one of the oldest running businesses in town. This photograph shows the White House Restaurant in the early 1920s on the left hand side of Coast Highway before the road was paved. (Courtesy of the Laguna Beach Historical Society/ First American Title Corporation.)

Sylvia M. Klime, the mother of early homesteaders William and Nathaniel Brooks, is pictured around 1905. She was born June 2, 1826, and later lived in Laguna until her death on April 10, 1909. She was always willing to help those in need and in her life delivered over 300 babies as a mid-wife—and never charged anyone for the service. (Courtesy of the Ramsey Collection.)

Elmer Jahraus established a cigar factory in the Yoch Hotel two years after he came to Laguna in 1903. The cigars were shipped across the United States for select customers and were not locally consumed. In 1912, Jahraus opened the Lumberyard on Forest Avenue, which sped up the growth of the seaside community drastically. Before the Lumberyard was available, the nearest establishment to buy lumber was in Santa Ana. (Courtesy of the Ramsey Collection.)

Located at Victoria Beach, La Tour was built in 1926 by the Brown family with the purpose of providing a way to reach the beach from the high cliff houses above. The Victoria Beach Tower is a 60-foot, Norman-style tower with a staircase inside. (Courtesy of Silver Images.)

Pyne Castle is a three-story, Normandy Revival–style mansion located at 770 Hillcrest Drive. When the 62-room building was constructed in the mid-1920s, owner Walter Pyne originally named the large home Broad View Villa. Pyne owned the Pyne Piano Company in Santa Ana, and upon the mansion's completion, he moved 12 pianos into the home, though he only played the guitar. The property was bought in 1963, and the rooms were converted into apartments and have remained that way since. (Courtesy of the Ramsey Collection.)

Leo Wilson is pictured in front of his traveling grocery store, called "Stor-At-Dor," which was built from a Model T Ford by adding the cab in the back plus shelves within. Wilson would offer service every other day by alternating between the north and south of Laguna. Customers could actually walk into the truck and shop around the small traveling store. He offered food, water, and kerosene and even weighed new babies, at least for the three years that the store was mobile. (Courtesy of the Ramsey Collection.)

The Hemenway home was built in the 1890s with a large porch on which people would gather in the evening and dance. Hemenway was a leader of local affairs and was on the election and school boards. An expert blacksmith named "Old Dad" Fisher came to own the property, cut down eucalyptus trees, and covered the entire building with them. In the 1930s, it was a Native American art shop where one would find blankets hanging on rails outside. (Courtesy of the Ramsey Collection.)

Benjamin Handy, who was also known as "Uncle Benny," built the first cottage on the bluffs at the end of Legion Street and started the first Sunday school in his home. He is seen here preaching as he would on those Sundays. (Courtesy of the Ramsey Collection.)

Fred Aufdenkamp sits in front of his self-built log cabin around 1916. In 1915, he built a box ball alley on Forest Avenue as well as a movie theater next to it. He named it the Lynn Theater, after his son. In 1921, Fred built a second theater on Coast Highway that is still in use today. One of his log cabins became Laguna's first public library. (Courtesy of the Ramsey Collection.)

Lynn Aufdenkamp, son of Fred Aufdenkamp, sits at one of the family's many log cabins. Lynn manned the town's first radio station out of one of these log cabins and posted the latest news on a billboard outside for the townspeople to read. (Courtesy of the Ramsey Collection.)

Bruno Fulvio and his brother Dave came to Laguna to open their restaurant, which became Laguna Diner (pictured). Although the dining-car restaurant, located on Main Beach, was only around for less than five years, many celebrities graced its tables. It is said that Laguna local and actress Bette Davis often came for their great chili.

Violet Lansdell and her beloved dog Pepper stand in an Irvine lima bean field just outside of Laguna Beach. Residents of Laguna would go out to these lands just after they were harvested to glean the fields. (Courtesy of the Lansdell family.)

Claude Bronner built the White House Restaurant in 1918, making it one of the first restaurants in Laguna Beach. In 1936, he sold the business to a Mr. Bird. This photograph shows the well-known sign above the building that reads, "Let the Birds Feed You!" (Courtesy of Silver Images.)

Laguna Beach - 1936
PCH, Forest and Park Avenue

Girls in costume parade down the boardwalk in front of the Laguna Beach Hotel in the 1920s. (Courtesy of Silver Images.)

In 1936, brothers Van and Roy Childs opened the Pottery Shack, which would become one of Laguna's most famous retail sites. Later moved to the location of the previous Yum-Yum Tea Room on Brooks Street and South Coast Highway, the Pottery Shack quickly became an extremely popular location for tourists. The Pottery Shack also gave local pottery artists a place to showcase and sell their wares to the public. (Courtesy of the Laguna Beach Historical Society.)

RICHARD HALLIBURTON
MOYE STEPHENS

The Flying Carpet

Richard Halliburton was an adventurer, writer, charmer, world traveler, and resident of Laguna Beach. Upon graduating from Princeton in 1921, Halliburton rejected the conventional life of a job and family and instead went to Europe, where he and his college roommate rode bicycles through various countries, stopping to climb mountains, visit with leaders, gamble, and altogether see the sights. Halliburton made his way by selling the occasional travel story or charming his way onto trains and boats. In 1925, Halliburton's collection of stories from his travels after college, *The Royal Road to Romance*, became an immediate bestseller. Halliburton wrote of amazing and unusual adventures in far-off countries with humor and wit that also related to the average person. He continued traveling until his final adventure in March 1939, when he and his writing partner, Paul Mooney, traveled to China and boarded a recently commissioned 75-foot Chinese junk called the *Sea Dragon*. They were to write a new adventure tale of sailing this ship from Hong Kong to the Golden Gate International Exposition in San Francisco. The crew consisted of a hired captain, an engineer, a handful of young travelers, Mooney, and Halliburton. After three weeks at sea, the already failing ship struck a typhoon and was last seen battling mammoth waves about 2,800 miles away from its destination. After many days of extensive scouting, the search was called off and the crew presumed dead. In 1945, a rudder believed to have belonged to the *Sea Dragon* washed ashore in California. Although his young death is a great sadness, Halliburton was a great adventurer who perished doing exactly what he loved most. He is pictured here with the pilot of the *Flying Carpet*, Moye Stephens, who took Halliburton to seldom-visited places around the world for Halliburton's book named after the plane. (Courtesy of the Pancho Barnes Trust Estate Archive.)

63

In 1937, Halliburton commissioned a young architect, William Alexander Levy, to build a three-bedroom home for Halliburton, Levy, and Paul Mooney, who was Halliburton's travel partner, editor, and ghostwriter, as well as Levy's lover. The resulting house came to be known as the Hangover House, a European-inspired, modern masterpiece built of concrete, steel, and glass. The house's name had a dual meaning, because it seems to hang over the Aliso Canyon and is a reference to the frequent parties held there. Author Ayn Rand became friends with Levy and visited the house before writing *The Fountainhead*. In the book, Rand refers to the Heller House, which seems to be a thinly disguised version of the Hangover House. The beach in the lower left corner is Aliso Creek Beach. (Courtesy of Silver Images.)

Adventurer and author Richard Halliburton drives pilots Moye Stephens (left) and "Pancho" Barnes (right). (Courtesy of the Pancho Barnes Trust Estate Archive.)

A group of Laguna thespians gathered in a living room in 1920 to discuss the need to establish a community theater. In 1924, the Laguna Playhouse was built on Ocean Avenue in downtown Laguna Beach. Although it was relocated in 1969 to the Moulton Theatre, located on the Laguna Canyon Road, the callboard still stands on Ocean Avenue as a reminder of the original location. (Courtesy of the Ramsey Collection.)

The Sandwich Mill restaurant sits on the corner of Forest Avenue and Coast Highway, as seen here in 1931. Frank Cuprien originated the round table where artists and writers would meet to talk about Laguna and art-related topics. Bing Crosby was known to stop at the Sandwich Mill before going to the Del Mar racetracks. (Courtesy of the Laguna Beach Historical Society/First American Title Corporation.)

The Laguna Beach Lifeguard Tower was built in the 1920s and used as a Union Oil filling station on the southeast corner of Broadway Street and Pacific Coast Highway until the early 1930s. (Courtesy of the Laguna Beach Historical Society/First American Title Corporation.)

A view from the north, above Broadway Street, shows the lifeguard tower in use as a Union Oil filling station in the early 1930s. The white structure to the bottom right is the Pomona College Marine Laboratory. (Courtesy of the Marriner family.)

The Spanish-styled station was offered to the Laguna Beach lifeguards by Union Oil Company in 1932. The city accepted the gift, and the structure was moved in 1932 to its current location on Main Beach. The building is now the town's most photographed structure. (Courtesy of Silver Images.)

This Coast Highway building sat between Oak and Brooks Streets, where it served as various car dealerships until the 1960s. The photograph dates to around 1939. (Courtesy of Silver Images.)

The building pictured was constructed in 1917 on North Coast Highway, where it has been used as the Cottage Restaurant since 1964. Early Laguna Beach developer and civic leader Joe Skidmore lived in the building and named it Sans Souci. This photograph was taken in the early 1920s. (Courtesy of the Laguna Beach Historical Society.)

The construction of motion picture director Edward H. Griffith's Three Arch Bay pool is seen here in 1929. Griffith directed many silent films. (Courtesy of the Turnbull Collection.)

A young class of El Moro students is pictured here with the Laguna Beach Fire Department in the mid-1950s. (Courtesy of the Brown family.)

Sprouse-Reitz Stores was founded in Portland, Oregon, in 1909. This Sprouse-Reitz was located on Broadway Street in downtown Laguna Beach. (Courtesy of the Laguna Beach Historical Society/ First American Title Corporation.)

Laguna's first greeter, Old Joe Lucas, would stand at the Isch general store, where he greeted visitors who came in on the Concord Stage. Pictured here in 1908, Old Joe Lucas is holding his well-known trident. (Courtesy of the Laguna Beach Historical Society.)

The Isch general store, which included Laguna's first post office, was located across the street from the current Hotel Laguna on Pacific Coast Highway and Laguna Avenue. Storeowner Nick Isch often went out in the middle of the day to fish and would leave the door open so that customers could help themselves while he was gone. (Courtesy of the Laguna Beach Historical Society.)

The Laguna greeter, Eiler Larsen, is seen here welcoming drivers and visitors in one of his usual spots on the Coast Highway. Larsen would wave and holler a big "Helloo!" to those passing by. (Courtesy of Silver Images.)

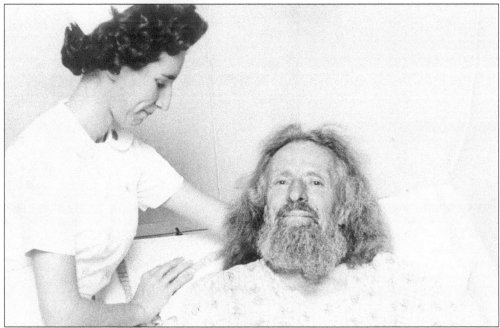

Eiler Larsen's health began to fade in the mid-1960s, but he continued to greet visitors when he was able. In 1972, Larsen wanted to visit the Sawdust Festival one last time. He was guided through the show on a stretcher and was able to enjoy the art festival a last time before his death in 1975. (Courtesy of Silver Images.)

In memory of Laguna's very special greeter, Eiler Larsen, two large statues were placed in town. The one seen here shows the statue on South Coast Highway in front of the Pottery Shack, which is now the Old Pottery Place. (Courtesy of Silver Images.)

The Villa Rockledge was built from 1918 through 1921 and is one of Laguna's famous structures. The home was constructed by the owner of the historic Mission Inn located in Riverside, California, Frank Miller, who originally called it Mariona after his second wife, Marion. The cliff-side home was built entirely by hand and was added onto and perfected until the late 1920s. (Courtesy of the Roger Jones Collection.)

A view of the entrance of Villa Rockledge shows a sign above the entranceway that reads "Mariona," the original name of the home. The architecture of the building was inspired by Mediterranean and Spanish styles. (Courtesy of the Roger Jones Collection.)

Villa Rockledge and Riverside, California, Mission Inn developer Frank Miller stands on the rocks near his cliff-side home with his grandchildren Frank (left) and Isabella Hutchings (right). (Courtesy of the Roger Jones Collection.)

Dedicated Laguna historian Merle Ramsey inspects a well in the Laguna Canyon. (Courtesy of the Ramsey Collection.)

Early settler John Damron homesteaded a large area of town in 1878 that included what is now Temple Hills. The property was purchased by George Rogers in the 1890s for $1,000 and was then subdivided into lots. The picture shows the Temple Hills area in the 1930s. (Courtesy of the Laguna Beach Historical Society/First American Title Corporation.)

The home and studio of early Laguna artist Frank Cuprien was located near Bluebird Canyon. Cuprien's home was known as the "Viking House." Upon his death in 1948, Cuprien left his estate to the Laguna Beach Art Association, an organization of which he had been a member of since its beginnings in 1918. (Courtesy of Silver Images.)

Forty-year Laguna Beach resident Jack Norworth wrote the classic sports song "Take Me Out to the Ball Game." Jack Norworth and his wife, Amy, hand out Cracker Jacks to young baseball players in this photograph. (Courtesy of the Laguna Beach Historical Society.)

Richard Nixon stops at Laguna Beach City Hall in 1952, when he was Dwight D. Eisenhower's vice presidential running mate on the Republican ticket. Here he speaks to Laguna residents. Orange County native Nixon was eventually elected president in 1968. (Courtesy of the Laguna Beach Historical Society.)

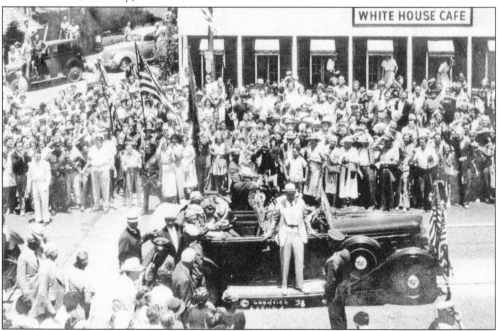

On July 16, 1938, Pres. Franklin D. Roosevelt drove though Laguna Beach as part of a parade. President Roosevelt can be seen here waving from the back of the car on the left side. (Courtesy of the Laguna Beach Historical Society.)

Four

ART, FESTIVALS, AND FILMS

Used from 1918 to 1929

As people discovered the town and word began to spread of Laguna's vast and diverse beauty, it was only natural that artists started moving to and visiting the seaside village. Laguna's very first art gallery opened on July 27, 1918, next to what is now the Hotel Laguna on Coast Highway. Over 300 spectators came on that opening day, and within the next month, around 2,000 people had visited the small gallery. Featured in the building was work from 25 artists with about 100 oil and watercolor paintings as well as some sculptures. This was the first big step in proclaiming Laguna as an artist colony. (Courtesy of the Laguna Beach Historical Society.)

Plein air artist Edgar Payne was born in Washburn, Missouri, on March 1, 1882. Payne moved to Laguna Beach in 1917 and within a year led efforts to open Laguna Beach's first art gallery, later known as the acclaimed Laguna Art Museum. The month after the gallery opened, he founded the Laguna Beach Art Association and served as the first president. At the time, there were only a few art galleries in California, making Laguna Beach an unwitting forefather in creating the state's artistic climate. Payne met photographer George Hurrell in 1925 at the Art Institute of Chicago and commissioned him to come to Laguna Beach to photograph the art colony. This photograph of Payne and the following photographs of other art association members were the products of Hurrell's visit. (Courtesy of the Laguna Art Museum/Gift of J. T. Bird/Photograph by George Hurrell.)

Coastal and landscape impressionist Anna Hills was born on January 28, 1882, in Ravenna, Ohio. After moving to Laguna Beach in 1912, Anna became a leader of the art community in the town. After helping Payne establish the first art gallery in Laguna Beach, Anna was Laguna Beach Art Association president from 1922 to 1925 and again from 1927 to 1930. Anna taught art, gave lectures, held exhibitions, and strongly encouraged the teaching of visual arts in public schools. Anna's plein air subjects included deserts, canyons, missions, and seas. (Courtesy of the Laguna Art Museum/Gift of J. T. Bird/Photograph by George Hurrell.)

Known as the "Dean of Southern California artists," William Wendt was a distinguished Laguna artist who was born on February 20, 1865, in Bentzen, Germany. Wendt built his home in Laguna Beach in 1913 and settled here permanently with his wife, sculptress Julia Bracken. (Courtesy of the Laguna Art Museum/Gift of J. T. Bird/Photograph by George Hurrell.)

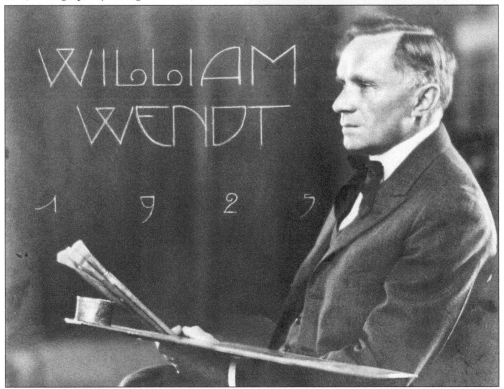

Frank Cuprien was born in Brooklyn, New York, on August 23, 1871, and was drawn to the beauty of the sea from a young age. In 1912, Cuprien came to Laguna Beach and stayed for the rest of his life. Cuprien help found the town's first art gallery and was president of Laguna Beach Art Association from 1921 to 1922. He knew that it was important to support and preserve art in Laguna for the future of the town. His art strongly focused on marine and coastal scenes with dramatic lighting. (Courtesy of the Laguna Art Museum/Gift of J. T. Bird/Photograph by George Hurrell.)

Plein air artist William Griffith was born in Lawrence, Kansas, on August 19, 1866. In 1918, Griffith came to Laguna Beach to visit a friend named Benjamin Chambers Brown while on sabbatical from Kansas University, where he had taught for over 20 years. In 1920, Griffith moved to Laguna Beach, where he became an active member of the Laguna Beach art community and worked in oils and pastels. Griffith became president of the Laguna Beach Art Association from 1920 to 1921 and 1925 to 1927. (Courtesy of the Laguna Art Museum/Gift of J. T. Bird/Photograph by George Hurrell.)

Frank Cuprien is seen riding on the right side of this float with some lovely mermaid sirens. (Courtesy of the Laguna Beach Historical Society.)

This float was Laguna Beach's entry in the 1936 Tournament of Roses in Pasadena, where it won first prize. (Courtesy of Silver Images.)

A parade marches through downtown Laguna Beach in the 1930s. (Courtesy of Silver Images.)

Carl "Pop" Abel, a local contractor and woodcarver, worked on local pieces such as Jolly Roger and Pottery Shack woodcarvings. Abel also ran the Woodcarving School, pictured here, which is still located across the street from Mozambique in between Agate and Pearl Streets. (Courtesy of Greg Abel.)

Durlin Brayton attended the Art Institute of Chicago and began his pottery making in Laguna Beach in 1928. He effectively established art pottery in the town by making handcrafted vases, lamps, and dinnerware in a small kiln. After World War II, business began to decline, and in 1968, his pottery business closed. (Courtesy of Silver Images.)

This is an early view of the Laguna Art Center. (Courtesy of Silver Images.)

Isaac Jenkinson Frazee was the creator of the Native American pageant *Kitshi Manido*. (Courtesy of the Laguna Beach Historical Society.)

Kitshi Manido, the town's first pageant, was held in 1921 in a eucalyptus grove in Sleepy Hollow on Catalina Street and Arroyo Chico. Frazee, its creator, came to know Native Americans while traveling to California in the 1870s. He was inspired by them to create this pageant depicting their lives. He and his wife traveled to the home of the Pala Indians to create authentic costumes for the performance. Many of the townspeople worked on this pageant to create the lighting, sets, costumes, and publicity. The money from the pageant was to be used to fund a fireproof art gallery for the local and visiting artists to exhibit their work. (Courtesy of the Laguna Beach Historical Society/Tom Pulley Postcard Collection.)

84

The building of the Festival of Arts and Pageant of the Masters is pictured on the organization's permanent grounds in the Laguna Canyon around 1941. The first Festival of Arts and Pageant of the Masters was held on the newly constructed site from June 30 to July 8, 1941, and was a huge success. (Courtesy of the Festival of Arts.)

The Irvine Bowl is where the Pageant of the Masters is held every summer. James Irvine donated a small area in the canyon for the pageant, and the space was dedicated to him. (Courtesy of the Festival of Arts/Laguna Beach Library Postcard Collection.)

In 1935, Roy Ropp developed the origins of the Pageant of the Masters into its present-day format. Ropp renamed the new and improved event "The Spirit of the Masters" and continued to design and produce it with resounding success until 1941. In 1936, the production was renamed the Pageant of the Masters. (Courtesy of the Laguna Beach Historical Society.)

Thousands of people come every year to view the work displayed at the Festival of Arts at the mouth of the Laguna Canyon. (Courtesy of the Festival of Arts/Laguna Beach Library Postcard Collection.)

Whistler's Mother was recreated with a live person for the 1933 Pageant of the Masters. (Courtesy of the Festival of Arts.)

Presenting the recreation of Leonard da Vinci's *The Last Supper* is a tradition at the Pageant of the Masters and has concluded the show nearly every year of operation since 1936. (Courtesy of the Festival of Arts.)

Thomas Gainsborough's *The Blue Boy* is another favorite at the Pageant of the Masters. (Courtesy of the Festival of Arts.)

The Pageant of the Masters has presented many of the great renowned artworks through the years, such as the *Sistine Madonna* by Raphael. (Courtesy of the Festival of Arts.)

The living version of local artist Ken Auster's silk-screen collage *Pier Shot* is reproduced with live models in the Pageant of the Masters. (Courtesy of the Festival of Arts/Laguna Beach Library Postcard Collection/Photograph by Lang Photography.)

On the left is a reproduction of the original pastel sketch of Toulouse-Lautrec's favorite model, and on the right is the finished print poster, entitled *Jane Avril Dancing at Jardin de Paris* by Henri Toulouse-Lautrec in the Pageant of the Masters. (Courtesy of the Festival of Arts/Laguna Beach Library Postcard Collection.)

A Pageant of the Masters presentation reproduced a watercolor and pastel piece called *Saturday Matinee*, seen here, originally painted by Laguna artist Sally Strand. (Courtesy of the Festival of Arts/Laguna Beach Library Postcard Collection/Photograph by Lang Photography.)

Some of the Sawdust members are found here painting a Sawdust Festival sign in 1968. The woman in the center is Dolores Ferrell, who was on the festival's board of directors. This was the first year the Sawdust Festival was held at its present-day Laguna Canyon address. (Courtesy of Silver Images.)

The Sawdust Festival broke away from the Festival of Arts in 1965, and some others also formed the Art-A-Fair. The first Sawdust Festival only featured a few dozen people, and it was held at the bottom of Park Avenue in an empty lot. (Courtesy of Silver Images.)

Eiler Larsen greets a young girl at the Sawdust Festival. (Courtesy of Silver Images.)

After George
Hurrell came to
Laguna Beach
to photograph
the artists
of the town,
he decided
to move to
California in
order to pursue
his painting
career and
ended up
finding more
work shooting
portraits. Andy
Warhol and
George Hurrell
are pictured
later on in
Hurrell's career.
(Courtesy of
the George
Hurrell Estate.)

Pancho Barnes was brave and clever—a rebel and a tomboy. She was one of only two dozen aviatrixes in the United States at the time and flew so well that she even beat Amelia Earhart's woman's world speed record. Born in 1901 as Florence Lowe, Pancho received her nickname while disguised as a man in Mexico, roaming the country on donkey-back with an acquaintance who called her Pancho after the sidekick character of Sancho Panza from *Don Quixote*. She inherited her mother's home in North Laguna, where she had wild parties and built a runway for flying to and from her Cliffside home. Hurrell took this portrait to show that he could portray the rugged Barnes as a glamorous beauty. (Courtesy of the Pancho Barnes Trust Estate Archive.)

One of the first people George Hurrell met and photographed in California was the headstrong aviatrix Pancho Barnes. The two became close friends, and she introduced Hurrell to some of her glamorous friends, like actor Ramon Novarro, who also had Hurrell take portraits of him. Novarro was so pleased with his photographs that he showed them to coworkers at MGM studios, where they quickly made their way to Norma Shearer, who enjoyed their sultry and sophisticated quality. Shearer commissioned Hurrell to take her portrait to convince her husband, MGM producer Irving Thalberg, to cast her as the sexy lead role in the upcoming *The Divorcee*. The photographs were taken, Shearer got the lead, and Hurrell became MGM's official portrait photographer. Hurrell's style became the standard of the 1930s glamour look, and he went on to shoot many famous people. All the while, George and Pancho remained friends, and when it came time to send away for her pilot's license from Orville Wright, she had Hurrell take somewhat masculine photographs so that she would not be turned down for being a woman. (Courtesy of the Pancho Barnes Trust Estate Archive.)

Photographer William Mortensen moved to Laguna Beach in 1931 and opened his studio that same year. His *Self Portrait as a Magician* is seen here. (Courtesy of the Center for Creative Photography.)

William Mortensen Studio was at 903 South Coast Highway at Thalia Street. The building is now the very popular Thalia Street Surf Shop. (Courtesy of the Center for Creative Photography.)

William Mortensen's photography school brochure features one of his most famous photographs on the cover. In Moretensen's time of teaching classes in Laguna Beach, around 3,000 people studied under him and learned his scientific and artistic photography techniques. (Courtesy of the Laguna Beach Historical Society.)

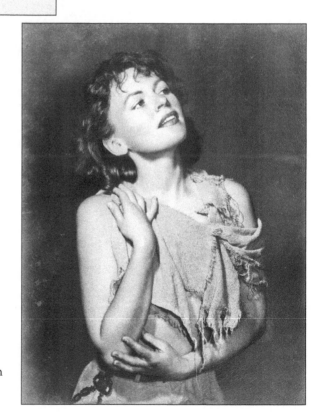

Vanity in Rags by William Mortensen is seen here. (Courtesy of the Laguna Beach Historical Society.)

This is the Shell Cove movie set in Three Arch Bay for *Give Us This Night* (1936), featuring Sidney Toler and Alan Mowbray. (Courtesy of the Karen Turnbull Collection/The Laguna Beach Public Library.)

A closer look shows the Three Arch Bay film set for *Give Us This Night*, which was set in an Italian fishing village. (Courtesy of the Karen Turnbull Collection/The Laguna Beach Public Library.)

An unidentified man poses
for a snapshot in front of the
massive film prop located
on a beach in Laguna.
(Courtesy of Silver Images.)

Beachgoers explore a boat that was used for a film on shore in Laguna Beach. (Courtesy
of Silver Images.)

A film set at Aliso Beach is pictured in the 1920s. (Courtesy of the Karen Turnbull Collection/ The Laguna Beach Library.)

This movie set was in Fisherman's Cove, but the name of the movie is unknown. The only clue is the sign on the boat that reads "Jonah's Retreat." (Courtesy of the Laguna Beach Historical Society.)

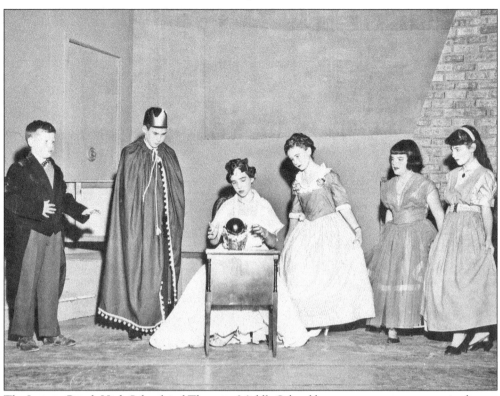

The Laguna Beach High School and Thurston Middle School have very strong programs in theater and constantly produce impressive and well-made plays. (Courtesy of the Brown family.)

The Laguna Beach Art Museum is the product of the very first 1918 art gallery, which was created by the Laguna Beach Art Association. (Courtesy of Silver Images.)

Five

BEACHES AND NATURE

Laguna Beach is home to many beautiful and unique beaches. The rugged coast creates many small and often secluded beaches. Government protections have been placed on many locations in the Laguna area to preserve nature from constant tourism. The beaches are protected by marine acts and are also cared for by many private associations. Laguna is something special among the rest of Orange County's coastal communities in that the breathtaking surroundings receive extraordinary care. (Courtesy of Silver Images.)

Goff Island is set between Treasure Island Beach and Victoria Beach. The "island" is the rock formation named after early Laguna Settler Hubbard Goff, who built the Arch Beach Hotel. (Courtesy of Silver Images.)

This hut built in Boat Canyon was constructed by two fishermen around 1913, which most likely led to the naming of the beach as Fisherman's Cove. The area is a marine preserve that is good for observing octopus, lobsters, and various crabs within its rock reef environment. (Courtesy of Silver Images.)

In order to keep Laguna wilderness preserved and full of the nature that makes it so pleasant, many active locals have created conservation groups that over the years have successfully preserved much of the land in the Laguna Canyon, including the only natural lakes in all of Orange County. (Courtesy of Silver Images.)

Creating sandcastles is a traditional activity at any beach. This line of castles is seen at Fisherman's Cove in the 1950s. (Courtesy of the Brown family.)

This early photograph of Diver's Cove in the 1920s shows the area without any of the numerous houses that now line the beachside cliffs. The area is home to many small sharks and rays as well as the visiting sea lion. (Courtesy of Silver Images.)

The El Morro Village Trailer Park stood between Laguna Beach and Newport Coast since the 1930s and is depicted here in 1948. Vacationers used to set up camp for however long they wanted in El Morro Canyon, and ones who decided to stay fulltime would pay their rents to the Irvine Company. In 1979, the State of California bought around 3,000 acres of land, including El Morro Park, which was earmarked for conversion into Crystal Cove State Park. In 2004, the residents had to begin to leave so that work creating the park could continue. (Courtesy of the Laguna Beach Historical Society.)

These three girls are enjoying the whimsical qualities of the beach sand. The "headstone" says, "Who will take my place? I am gone." (Courtesy of the Brown family.)

Heisler Park is a half-mile long recreation area along beachside cliffs in North Laguna. The park includes gardens, walking paths, beach access, and picnic areas, as seen here. (Courtesy of the Brown family.)

Rockpile Beach is located along Heisler Park, near Main Beach, and is one of three designated surfing areas of Laguna Beach. (Courtesy of the Marriner family.)

A slightly more serene Main Beach is pictured here at night. (Courtesy of the Marriner family.)

A beautiful view of Aliso Creek is seen here at its mouth, where it empties into the sea out of Aliso Canyon. This is where the Thurston family first homesteaded in 1871. (Courtesy of the Marriner family.)

A man enjoys the view of Arch Beach and the Pacific Ocean from this nearby cliff. (Courtesy of the Marriner family.)

Aliso Beach has been a very popular stop for beachgoers from the beginning of tourism in Laguna. It was a privately operated campground until the County of Orange obtained the land in the 1960s and installed various facilities including a pier in 1971. Aliso Beach is one of the easier beaches to access due to its large parking lot and wide, open shore. The beach is still extremely popular today and yearly hosts the highly respected skimboarding contest, the Victoria Skimboards Pro/Am. (Courtesy of the Marriner family collection.)

Crescent Bay is a spacious and popular beach that is located in the area of North Laguna and named for its crescent-moon-like shape. Attracting many visitors in the summer because of its diverse conditions, the beach is a desirable destination for fishing, diving, skimboarding, and sunbathing. (Courtesy of the Marriner family collection.)

The north end of Victoria Beach once had a pool built into the rock. (Courtesy of the Laguna Beach Historical Society.)

ARCH BEACH, LAGUNA BEACH, CALIFORNIA

This postcard features Arch Beach. (Courtesy of the Phillips family.)

This photograph shows two of the three arches in Three Arch Bay in 1978. (Courtesy of the Karen Turnbull Collection/ The Laguna Beach Library.)

This photograph of Three Arch Bay, taken in 1978, shows the community members' boats along the shore as well as Whale Island in the center. (Courtesy of the Karen Turnbull Collection/The Laguna Beach Library.)

The town of Laguna Beach has been no stranger to natural disasters in recent years, and even back in 1926, the town had to deal with flooding, as seen in this photograph taken on what is now Coast Highway. Since then, the small town has survived fires, floods, mudslides, hurricanes, and waterspouts. (Courtesy of Silver Images.)

Many piers have been erected in Laguna since the early days of the town, and they have one by one all succumbed to large storms and waves. The pier at Heisler Park stood for 43 years before a hurricane hit on September 24, 1939, and destroyed the pier. (Courtesy of Silver Images.)

Large waves crash on Main Beach near the Hotel Laguna. (Courtesy of Silver Images.)

Teenagers in the 1970s growing up in Laguna began to take skimboarding seriously as a sport and wanted others to know about it as well. Local boarders Tex Haines and Peter Prietto started a skimboard company called Victoria Skimboards, which has grown to be a successful and respected business. Mark MacRae is seen skimboarding at Brooks Street Beach in July 1965. (Courtesy of the MacRae Collection.)

Lifeguard George Griffith, son of Laguna plein air artist William Griffith, is seen in one of the very first images of skimboarding. Using a board called an Auquaslide—developed by Evinrude to be sold with their outboard motors and boats for use as a tow behind the boat—Griffith skimboards across Main Beach in 1929. (Courtesy of Victoria Skimboards.)

Mark MacRae gets ready to use his surfboard at Brooks Street Beach in 1965. Brooks Street Beach is a surfing beach that is located between Oak and Cress Street Beaches to the south of Main Beach. (Courtesy of the MacRae Collection.)

Bud MacRae catches a wave on his surfboard at Oak Street Beach in October 1966. (Courtesy of the MacRae Collection.)

When the waves were flat, kids had the popular skateboards to "sidewalk surf" with, as seen on Thalia Street in 1965. (Courtesy of the MacRae Collection.)

These beach-bathing women are using some handy bathing suit changing bags at Three Arch Bay. (Courtesy of the Karen Turnbull Collection/The Laguna Beach Library.)

Six

SCHOOLS, CHURCHES, CLUBS, AND TEAMS

The second- through fourth-grade students in 1926 show their costumes off at the May Day pageant at the one-room school on Park Avenue before the high school was built. (Courtesy of the Laguna Beach Historical Society.)

The third school in Laguna was built on Park Avenue in 1908 on the site of the old cemetery. This two-room school became too small and was moved down the hill to its present location, where it is used as the Legion Hall. When grading the road for the next school in 1928, the grave of Capt. Oliver Brooks was accidentally unearthed, and students began gathering the bones as souvenirs. The bones were regained and moved to a cemetery in Santa Ana. The high school was finally completed in 1935. There are an estimated dozen graves still underneath the high school today. (Courtesy of Silver Images.)

The Laguna Beach eighth-grade class of 1933 is depicted here. (Courtesy of the Laguna Beach Historical Society.)

In 1935, Laguna Elementary School was relocated from its previous site on the current high school campus to a new location directly across the street. The building pictured here on Park Avenue is now the entrance building to the public swimming pool. (Courtesy of the Laguna Beach Historical Society.)

This aerial view of Laguna Beach High School was taken in the 1930s. (Courtesy of Silver Images.)

Susie Brown (second from left) sits with a teacher as she learns how to use the slide rule. Throughout the 1950s and 1960s, the slide rule regained popularity as a "modern tool," and little Susie Brown was even featured on television for her knowledge of its use. (Courtesy of the Brown family.)

The view from Laguna Beach High School's field is one to be jealous of. St. Ann's Drive runs behind the high school track and field. (Courtesy of Silver Images.)

Hal Akins was head coach of the football team in the 1960s. He was a sportsman and also an artist. Akins worked with mixed media and later had a booth at the Sawdust Art Festival. (Courtesy of the Lansdell family.)

Laguna Beach High School cheerleaders show their school spirit in the early 1960s. (Courtesy of the Lansdell family.)

James "Wally" Lansdell is pictured as no. 21 in a football game at Laguna Beach High School's campus in the early 1960s. (Courtesy of the Lansdell family.)

The track teams from the 1940s through the mid-1960s had Olympic starter coach Red Guyer leading the team. Guyer field at Laguna Beach High School is named after the track coach. (Courtesy of the Lansdell family.)

The Laguna Beach High School marching band is pictured in their uniforms in the 1950s. (Courtesy of the Brown family.)

A troop of Girl Scouts enjoys the Aliso Canyon Elizabeth Dolph Girl Scouts Camp of Laguna Beach in the mid-1950s. (Courtesy of the Laguna Beach Historical Society.)

Laguna Beach Boy Scouts learn
how to greet with the peace sign.
Elmer Brown (left) and his son Doug
(second from right) are pictured.
(Courtesy of the Brown family.)

Boy Scout buddies of Laguna Beach smile for a quick snapshot. Doug Brown, who later
owned and operated Laguna Travel Service, is pictured at the bottom right. (Courtesy of
the Brown family.)

A group of five- and six-year-old girls take ballet lessons at Legion Hall in 1956. The girl pictured third from right is longtime Laguna resident Susan Gardner (then Susan Brown). Legion Hall was originally the two-room school built in 1908 on Park Avenue, which was later moved down the hill on Legion Street. (Courtesy of the Brown family.)

Members of the Little League baseball team of Laguna Beach pose together in the mid-1950s. Pictured here from left to right are (first row) unidentified, Usher Eason, Tim Cunningham, Jimmy Misner, and Jim Fanelli; (second row) Scott Cunningham, Steve Sherry, two unidentified, Bob Simpson, Ricky Balzer; (third row) Bill Santini, Ronald Palmer, Jerry Henry, Craig Dusenberry, Charles Trapp, Jimmy Allen, and Mr. Palmer. (Courtesy of Craig Dusenberry.)

Violet Lansdell (center) was very involved in the Women's Club and their activities, such as raising money for the city, Red Cross, and fund-raising for those in need. Lansdell was five times the president of the Women's Club in the 1950s and 1960s, helped raise money, for Bluebird Park and also mentored the Junior Women's Club members. (Courtesy of the Lansdell family.)

A group of families in town wanted a different kind of church in Laguna Beach, so they pooled their money and raised funds in order to buy some property for Calvary Evangelical Church. They eventually bought a property on Glennerye Street and started the church in October 1953. The church was there until 1960, and the property still stands today, now housing the Hare Krishna temple. The church and some of its members are pictured here in its early days in 1953. (Courtesy of the Lansdell family.)

St. Mary's Chapel and Harris Hall stand at the top of Park Avenue around 1927. (Courtesy of the Laguna Beach Historical Society.)

In the early days of the Laguna Beach Presbyterian Church, artists like Anna Hills and Frank Cuprien would teach through the church in classes such as Sunday school studies and music. In 1925, Raymond I. Brahams was installed as the pastor and proposed to build a Spanish Colonial sanctuary as it is today for $26,000. The grand building dwarfed all of the small wooden homes around it. The church is still in use today, but work is currently being done on the building to preserve and reinforce it. (Courtesy of the Laguna Beach Presbyterian Church Collection.)

Visit us at
arcadiapublishing.com

Lightning Source UK Ltd.
Milton Keynes UK
UKHW031011090223
416653UK00010B/407